GABBY

The Vampire Cabbie

For Stan Cohen
J. W.

For the Mitchell Family, Klub Barbounia members
K. P.

ORCHARD BOOKS
96 Leonard Street, London EC2A 4XD
Orchard Books Australia
32/45-51 Huntley Street, Alexandria, NSW 2015
ISBN 1 84362 150 9 (hardback)
ISBN 1 84362 158 4 (paperback)
First published in Great Britain in 2004
First paperback publication in 2005
Text © Jeanne Willis 2004
Illustrations © Korky Paul 2004
A CIP catalogue record for this book is available
from the British Library.
1 3 5 7 9 10 8 6 4 2 (hardback)
1 3 5 7 9 10 8 6 4 2 (paperback)
Printed in Great Britain

GABBY

The Vampire Cabbie

Jeanne Willis * Korky Paul

ORCHARD BOOKS

GABBY

The Vampire Cabbie

Where do you want to go to, mate?
Up West? It's getting rather late.
I'm clocking off. You've got the fare?
All right, get in. I'll drive you there.

I've had 'em all inside my cab –
Vlad the Impaler, Mad Queen Mab.
I ran Cinderella home from the ball.
It's double the fare past midnight, an' all!

I drive a lot of witches - no broomsticks, see?
They can't fly their brooms without an M.O.T.
The covens get so crowded after dark –
They're better off by taxi - nowhere to park.

I've got all my regulars. Trade's very good –
I fetch Granny Riding Hood from the wood.
I take her to footy – it gives her a thrill
When big, bad Wolves are stuffed ten nil.

Ali Baba is in trouble - his carpet won't fly.
It's lost its magic but he doesn't know why.
I picked him up but he gave me lots of flannel -
"Your meter's wrong - it is cheaper by camel!"

11

The old Grim Reaper – he's good with his tips.

"You can't take it with you!" he always quips,

"Let's live dangerously...faster!" he'll cry.

"Hip hip hooray, we are going to die!"

I often get hailed by the Gingerbread Man.
He never stops running as fast as he can.
He beats everybody in the taxi queue –
And leaves crumbs on my back seat, too."

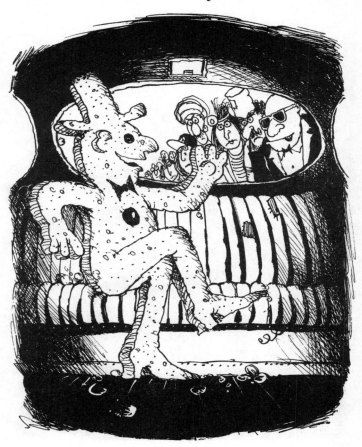

I once took some ghosts to a fair in the rain.
They wanted to go for a ride on a train.
"Off on your holidays?" "No!" they replied,
"Off to scare the 'orrible kids inside!"

The Trolls are a nuisance, they get a bit rough.
They often pick fights with the Billy Goats Gruff.
They always get injured and then phone me
To drive them to the Hospital. "Quick, A and E!"

I picked up a mummy one morning at four.
Its bandage got caught in the hinge of my door.
Then it unravelled and span out of sight.
I cursed it! I never got paid that night.

I get along fine with my fairyland clients,
Except, I'm afraid, with the Ogres and Giants.
They go to a pub and have too much to drink
Then they throw up - cor, it doesn't half stink!

The Headless Horseman freaked me out.
He stopped me at a roundabout.
The reason for my great alarm?
His head was underneath his arm!

He sat himself upon the seat
And put his head beside his feet.
"You can't put that down there, old fruit,"
I said, and slung it in the boot.

The head spoke back - I nearly died.
"Why shut me in the dark?" it cried.
"It's just a health and safety check,"
I said, "in case you break your neck."

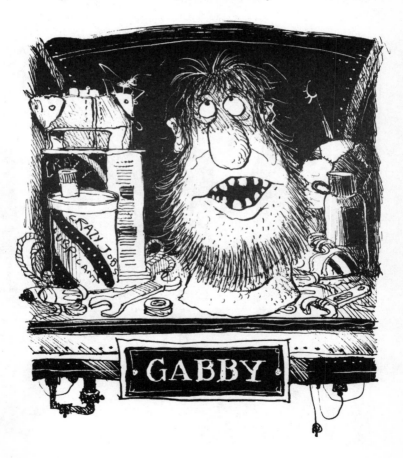

I had one pick-up some while back,
Smart young gentleman, dressed in black.
A very strong accent, too, he had.
He said he was a tourist from Leningrad.

He said, "I've not been well. I need
A bite or two! Yes, a good, long feed."
So I suggested to this charming bloke,
"How about a burger and a can of coke?"

His face looked awful - ghostly white.
I asked him if he felt all right.
"You look so pale and weak," I said.
He claimed he'd just got out of bed.

"Oh no, I can't eat that!" He sighed.
"I won't touch anything that's died.
I need something warm and red."
"The Curry House it is!" I said.

"Curry powder makes me sneeze,"
he said. I said, "So have Chinese!
I'll take you to the Foo Wong Lay,
They do a smashing take-away."

"I do not wish to go in there,"
he said. "I need some mountain air,
Please drive me to my castle first
Before I die of bloody thirst."

I didn't fancy that too much,
My cab had got a dodgy clutch.
My brakes weren't what they ought to be
And all those rocks were slippery.

The air was thick with fog and bats -
I felt too tired for friendly chats.
And when we'd only got halfway
The cab broke down. And no AA.

I radio'd to Cab Control:
"Yeah, Roger? I am in a hole."
But there was silence. Not a peep!
Control was home in bed, asleep.

In my rear mirror, I could see
This gentleman still watching me -
And he was gawping at my neck.
His fangs were showing! Flippin' heck!

"I'd offer you a drink," I said.
"Let's have a picnic here instead.
I'll get the rug out of the boot -
You mustn't spoil that lovely suit."

"That's very kind. I cannot wait!"
He smiled, "Don't bother with a plate,
I do not need a knife or fork -
My fangs could pierce a side of pork."

"I won't be long," I said. "Stay there,
Enjoy the view while I prepare
The perfect meal for us two chums,
Until the rescue service comes."

I took my thermos from the car,
And poured the contents in a jar.
I always carry it with me
In case a vampire comes to tea.

He took the drink. He drank it, "Cheers!"
The steam shot out of both his ears.
"That's not lemonade!" he swore.
"It's holy water! Please, no more!"

His throat was burning. Just for fun
I offered him a hot cross bun.
He saw the pastry crucifix
And screamed, "I beg you, no more tricks!"

"Oh dear," I said. "I thought I'd make
A lovely great big lump of STAKE!"
I waved my stick of pointed wood.
"No don't!" he screamed, "I will be good!"

But just to make sure I had won
I waved my copy of the *Sun*.
"Too bright!" he cried, and flew away
Back to his bat cave for the day.

"So long, Sucker – off you go!
You can't get blood from me, you know."
What's more, he'd left his mobile phone!
I called a cab to take me home.

Written by Jeanne Willis * Illustrated by Korky Paul

Jeff the Witch's Chef	1 84362 146 0
Lillibet the Monster Vet	1 84362 145 2
Norman the Demon Doorman	1 84362 159 2
Vanessa the Werewolf Hairdresser	1 84362 148 7
Annie the Gorilla Nanny	1 84362 155 X
Gabby the Vampire Cabbie	1 84362 158 4
Bert the Fairies' Fashion Expert	1 84362 149 5
Iddy Bogey, the Ogre Yogi	1 84362 160 6

All priced at £3.99 each

Crazy Jobs are available from all good book shops, or can be ordered direct
from the publisher: Orchard Books, PO BOX 29, Douglas IM99 1BQ
Credit card orders please telephone 01624 836000
or fax 01624 837033 or visit our Internet site: www.wattspub.co.uk
or e-mail: bookshop@enterprise.net for details.

To order please quote title, author and ISBN
and your full name and address.
Cheques and postal orders should be made payable to 'Bookpost plc.'
Postage and packing is FREE within the UK
(overseas customers should add £1.00 per book).
Prices and availability are subject to change.